I, Little Asylum

Originally published as *La petite Borde.* © Mercure de France, 2012.
This translation © 2014 by Semiotext(e).

Published by Semiotext(e)
2007 Wilshire Blvd., Suite 427, Los Angeles, CA 90057
www.semiotexte.com

Thanks to Noura Wedell and Erik Morse.

Design by Hedi El Kholti
ISBN: 978-1-58435-137-5

Distributed by The MIT Press, Cambridge, Mass. and London,
England

I, Little Asylum

Emmanuelle Guattari

Translated by E.C. Belli

semiotext(e)

CONTENTS

To Hugo, Élie, and Gisèle
For Nicolas

I

MY BROTHER

Scumbag!

Hick!

"Manou, are you asleep?"

"You know, your tonsils are going to get bigger and bigger and then you'll die."

"I'm telling Dad!"

"Jump!"

"No."

"Do it! Jump!"

"No."

"I'll give you five francs if you jump."

So I jumped.

"See, look, you're swimming! Come on, keep going!" my brother said.

I sank.

My brother jumped in after me. But I still swallowed a whole lot of water.

Then, that hypocrite said, "Aren't you happy, my little Manou? You won five francs! Here, I'll give them to you right away. What are you going to buy, huh? Candy? You won't tell Dad, right?"

"Jump!"
"No!"
"Jump! Come on! Hurry! Go, now! Or it'll be too late."

So I jumped off the motorcycle.

"There you go! It's not so bad, see! You rolled. You won't hurt yourself that way. Get it? Roll off your shoulder, that's how stuntmen do it. Like that! Are you scared? Don't be. Let's do it again."

My brother would even jump off of trains when he missed the Blois stop.

I'm in the forest walking behind my brother. It's very early and chilly. He keeps looking back at me, annoyed. "Shut up and be quiet!"

He stops and explains, "That's not how you're supposed to walk. If you don't want the twigs to crack, you need to put the ball or heel of your foot down *first* and *then* the rest. But most important, keep your mouth shut!"

We move along the marshy edges of the pond where the birds nest. We proceed in silence, our boots treading the water, which is, at first, up to what must be my brother's ankles and my knees as we make our way around the little heaps the gorse forms. I am so focused on what I must do with my feet that when the water reaches my waist I hardly notice. I slip into a hole, soundlessly. The water's now at my chin. I make a little lapping sound with my hands. My brother turns around and grabs me by the collar.

"Oh, my poor little Manou!"

THE MONKEY

We had a monkey. My father brought it back from Africa.

One day, he opened his jacket and the monkey was there, inside, tiny and cowering against him.

It became quite fat. Its name was Boubou. It was light beige. *It* was a female.

She loved our father. She hated the three of us though.

She thought our father was her mother.

She was like some pet dog around him. She searched his hair for lice.

She snarled at us the minute he'd look away.

We tried telling him.

But he never believed us:

"Boubou is a doll," he'd say.

She really became quite fat.

My father had a perch and chain set up for her in the entrance.

My father would always walk in first; we'd follow.

That's where we had to leave our shoes. There, where Boubou would melt onto us and claw at our skulls.

We ended up designating one of us, in turn: "It's *you* Boubou's attacking today."

The rest would run off, leaving a heap of shoes behind.

One day, my father announced to us that Boubou had escaped with her chain.

For a long time my father searched for her; he called for her outside, *Bou-bou, Bou-bou!*

Months passed.

Then, my father told us he had some bad news.

A deep white skeleton with a chain had been found inside a tree.

We would have liked to see it, but we never found the spot.

LA CHAUFFE

'La Chauffe,' the transportation office, often organized our ride to school, meaning that a resident would pick us up in one of those Citroën 2CVs owned by La Borde.

We'd meet the car and its driver in front of the castle.

We piled up in the back, the littler ones in the laps of the older ones, our mouths and hands glued to the cold tube formed by the rear bench seat.

For a long time, it was Alexandre who came. He drove very, very slow. We kept relatively quiet.

We'd watch the speedometer. Whenever he reached 20km/hour, he lifted his foot off the gas pedal; I don't think he ever shifted into second. The motor's deafening throb made for a monotonous ride along the vineyards and the woodlands. We often got bored, especially when he drove up the hill. But we were never late. The main attraction of our ride was that Alexandre would always let go of the steering wheel to scratch the palm of his hand with his opposite hand, and we'd try to count at what interval.

He was very kind to us. There were other pricklier residents, and around them, we kept a low profile.

He'd unload us in front of the school like we were some big warm batch of baked goods.

We were the kids from La Borde.

In the early sixties, for the village of Cour-Cheverny, the Clinic was still some sort of fantastical presence. The fear of the *Insane* was palpable. And fear is what logically made of us birds of a feather, a merry band of oddballs who let Madmen roam about freely in a fenceless park and lived among them, too. I took note of this state of affairs when I first began pre-school.

In the vibrant and wholesome universe of the Labordian phalanstery into which we'd been born, I'd never been able to take full stock of the situation.

We knew, of course, that the Residents were Madmen. But La Borde was, first and foremost, our home.

We were not particularly aware of the Residents, whom we also called the Patients. They were simply there, and we were there too.

We felt affection toward some of them, and some of them liked us very much. But above all, in the eyes of the children that we were, they were grown-ups. And as such, they were bearers of a certain authority and were stronger; that was the chief difference between us and them.

We were often told not to disturb them, not to scream.

Otherwise, it seems to me that, just like the other children at La Borde, I naturally parsed, from my daily interactions, the madness from the most fundamentally human exchanges, which the whole project of La Borde protected fiercely, without one impinging on the other.

It was their aptitude for conversation, their care for others, their kindness or their impatience, the quality of their greeting, their aptitude for small talk, or to show genuine interest; the smiles, the insults, the absences and distractions, a worrisome or ravaged *faciality*, nervous behavior, atony or even catatony, the odd bodies, the gracious ones, the tortured hands, the outfits, the smells; as in any society, everything added up to some sort of signal which revealed whether contact was indeed possible; so, depending on the moment, we might have taken a sinuous little detour to avoid this or that Resident, or might have stopped them in their tracks and then returned to our child's play. Oftentimes, though, it was alone that we struck up a conversation with a Resident.

As a group, we were much too occupied.

And the Insane were often (as we were, but in their own way) quite busy too. Ultimately we lived in rather parallel universes, though in the same place. We barely skimmed each other.

Before too long, in fact, running in the castle was forbidden. We'd still try to do it quietly or pretend to, until they asked not to move around in groups anymore.

We were similarly forbidden from making any noise when we walked past the doctors' offices.

The notes that the Supervisors—who had patrolled the infirmary or done the night rounds—had taken down in their journals and that were shared each day in meetings would make their way down to us. *Madame This or Mister That is not doing very well today.*

Our father sometimes warned us about certain Residents: "A new Resident has just arrived. He does not like children. Do not go near him."

But most of the time we were elsewhere anyway. There was the vast immensity of the Park, the swamps, the pathways, the pond, the animals. And all the things which were forbidden.

After seven o'clock, when the bell rang at the Castle, announcing the Residents' dinnertime, it was officially evening at La Borde.

We'd all return home to our families for dinner. The housing for the staff and their families was very modest.

New Residents were always coming and room had to be made.

We went to bed at eight thirty. And the whole thing started again the next day.

And then one day the Comptroller showed up.

It was a word that was at once complicated (I was only four or five) and yet it was evocative enough.

And the effects of his action were so immediate and tangible that we quickly understood; before even having seen him, we'd imagined him tall and gaunt.

Whenever he went somewhere, consternated whispers followed him.

He could be seen, alone, striding the hallways toward the Commons, the Administrative Office, the Switchboard, the showers, the Chicken Coop; he was like a great scythe, demanding and radical; an austere reminder that the 'party' was over.

All of the little creature comforts, like the pink toilet paper, were gone. Erasers, Bic pens, all the little extras just snatched away from the community. Of course, there was still stealing.

THE KIDS FROM LA BORDE

We moved about like a host of sparrows, gathered in a brazen and loquacious constellation.

We went to the Castle.

We crossed the Grand Salon, snuck into the Dining Room and moved toward the Kitchen (or vice-versa) in long strands of children. We went to see René, the cook (my uncle); we'd always ask him for something.

We'd ask if we could help carry the big garbage containers to the pigs—the leftovers that were sorted after mealtimes, and the fruit and vegetable peels (and sometimes, randomly, other things too). The pigs had terrible little blue eyes. They'd try to eat any hand that lingered and, in the ruckus, crushed their younglings, who made high-pitched squeals.

If a Resident hadn't done it already, we'd carry the bucket full of soaked dry bread to the ducks in the pond.

We went fishing for whitebait in the Swamps.

We'd squeeze the slimmer kids in through the Castle's basement windows under the kitchen so they could bring us back bulk-sized cans of fruits in syrup (prunes or apricots) or chestnut cream, and off we went to hide.

There was also the car cemetery, in the Parking Lot near the entrance of the Clinic, on the path to the Chicken Coop. When it was raining, we sat in the bench seats and drove all afternoon, working the notched steering wheels and gearboxes of the old black Citroën Traction Avants, the Peugeot 403s, the Renault Dauphines, and Citroën DSes. They smelled like mold and motor oil.

In the fall, when the time for chestnut fights came again, we used the garbage can covers as shields. We had huge pitched battles, complete with black eyes and tears; we didn't always put the covers back.

We secretly smoked the cigarette butts that the Residents hadn't completely finished.

We went to the Chicken Coop to swallow raw eggs whole, stepping in the straw that we had climbed up.

We were allowed to attend the Workshops. We did pottery in the Big Glasshouse; we did sewing with Lala, whenever she set up a table outside, under the big Cedar near the chapel. We made garlands for the holidays. We went to Theater Workshop too.

We'd go see our parents, who worked at the Castle's or in the Park's Infirmaries, or where the dishes were being washed.

We'd say hello to the Residents; some of them sometimes gave us a franc to get a glass of soda from the Bar or to buy candy.

We were dressed up for fairs. We went to play in the empty booths and shacks that had been built and that were always left standing afterward.

At Christmas, there was a big tree in the Grand Salon and the children of the staff who stayed in their seats each received a gift.

We went to see the donkey, Tintin, near the sawmill. That's how we first came upon the pit.

Those who never saw La Borde's shit pit in person, under that open sky, cannot possibly fathom the extraordinary range of colors, shapes, and textures of that human creation. Our fascination, as children, with that giant pool, that huge sea of shit, made us defy all rules. Located at a distance, past the buildings of the sawmill, two basins, staring into the sky, held that astounding content. We climbed onto the narrow stone blocks that surrounded it and walked along carefully, following each other, babbling away and entertaining debates above that wild pile. We did this for quite a long time. Until one of us fell in. Then, shit pit times were over; aside from the strict orders we'd been given to stay away, they'd started a landfill project on it.

We'd known the old Childcare Center, a sort of large, plain room in the building behind the Clock Tower where they kept us before the age of two, before Preschool.

They built the new center in the meadow across the pond.

It was very striking, all made out of wood; massive trees grew through openings fashioned in the roof, and they lived in the Childcare Center like powerful, wrinkled elephant legs. The bathrooms were very small, like toys, and the kitchen table anchored into the ground was a height gauge of sorts. Once your knees touched your chin, your childhood was over.

The Childcare aimed to keep the children at somewhat of a distance from the Castle and life at the Clinic. Françoise Dolto had suggested it during a visit. And eventually, the children took on a more embarrassed attitude toward the Residents.

The first children of La Borde were already a bit older. So for them, a tutor was hired. Christian arrived. He was tall, handsome, athletic: a sort of demi-God.

We were caught in the woods, sitting cross-legged in a big circle on the cyclamen, passing around cigarettes we'd gathered. The one who caught us was as baffled as we were; the youngest were six.

The party was over.

Many families moved into town and settled there, in Blois.

THE TENCH

She didn't like rice. She didn't like sugar.

She drank Nescafé and smoked unfiltered Craven As. She'd told me: "I'll stop when the pack's five francs."

It wasn't true. She kept going until it was 15 francs, and then she died (the switch to the euro changed how things were priced; she'd been used to the system of old francs, and was rather approximate with new francs, to such an extent that I, who am speaking to you, was always a bit confused).

After visits to her doctor, she'd say: "I have nice pink lungs."

We called her The Tench because she loved to swim. She swam in the Beuvron. She swam up to the big buoy in the Mediterranean with this rhythmic little paddle, just like a frog.

She was very small. She'd lost all her teeth. Because of the war.

In a class photo from the end of primary school, she looks like she's six.

She had little square hands, very small, like those of a child.

She had Greek feet.

She had yellow skin and black hair. She told us that once upon a time, a rich young Arab man who was infatuated with her had asked her to marry him. She'd hesitated, but hadn't wanted to leave with him in the end.

She was very thin. She was flat chested.

She always bought fresh cream and butter, just in case. Because of the war.

She bought fresh milk, every day, just as you'd buy a newspaper.

On holiday, in Spain, she took us to gather snails from the cemeteries: women in black ran after us, scandalized.

She gathered shaggy ink caps laying around La Borde's dump site.

She never made cakes: "I don't like them," she'd tell us, with an expressive pout, to make it perfectly clear.

She made hard caramel, pouring it over marble slabs for it to cool, and gave it to us to suck on whenever she wanted to coax us into the bathtub.

She loved her little car. She drove fast.

Once a year, she bought medlar fruit.

She put oranges in the Christmas stockings along with our gifts.

She told us how she'd always wait too long before eating the one she received as a child, and how it would always rot. Then, she'd cry.

She hated rutabagas. Because of the war.

My mother has vanished from my life like a soap bubble that bursts.

Since then, I've been facing that new illusion.

Sometimes, I want to move my hand forward and beat the air to feel this strange new image.

How can it be? She was here. She isn't anymore. Where is she?

Then one day, as I peer at the avenue and the city through the window, the sky crashes into the ground.

It feels as though my head is in a vice, and a vertigo overtakes me: aren't our dead right there, behind that sort of screen, the one that lights up right before our eyes? I close my eyes. I shut my eyes tight. I wait. I open them again. No, I cannot see the dead. I look behind me too, but my mother is not there.

I say to myself, what if we could see the dead? How would we do it?

That's when the idea comes to me to ask if I can spend one more short moment with my mother.

So I ask the Administration of the Dead permission for a little time with my mother.

I'm not asking for much. Just fifteen minutes.

I tell myself to be persistent. So I ask again, every day.

I go and sit in a café, knowing she will come and sit across from me.

I am certain that she will come.

I'll give her two kisses hello; I'll hold her small stiff

hand a short while. She'll have that tense look, which her medications—as well as the world, which scared her—had brought over her. She'll have it not because of her visit from behind this veil of disappearance, but because she had already become that way.

I'm ready to make a deal with life: take ten years from me for a fifteen-minute conversation with her.

Take my eighties, take my seventies, Hell, take my sixties.

Give me back what you took! Give me a tiny instant of everything you robbed me of!

We'd meet in a café that would smell of cold cigarette, and there would be rain outside. On that fall night, the lights would glitter in the wet street.

We'd be sitting at a table next to a big window. She wouldn't have taken her coat off. She would have to go soon; and she would know it. But we wouldn't speak of it.

We'd sit there, stooped over the table.

Please, I beg you! I'd look at her one last time.

I go to the café every day and wait.

I sit there, leaning a bit into the fog on the window.

I'm sure they'll agree at some point.

My mother's memories of the Occupation never dulled.

She'd never made peace with it, and, refusing to embrace a modern Europe, she even continued to refer to 'the Krauts' (or 'the Heinies'), and would always jump nervously when she heard German being spoken around her. We never mentioned when our city became a sister city of Weimar, nor would I ever have dreamed of asking her to learn that language, although, quivering in the back bench-seat of the car, my cousins and I debated its usefulness should another war break out (against the Germans, undoubtedly, our imaginations told us).

To ensure that the memory of the war would live on, there suddenly appeared, at home, a collection of books on the atrocities of the camps, books which were left, curiously enough, fully accessible under the glass tray of the living room coffee table.

I was ten and I remember reading, with great concentration, the volume on the details of Mengele's experiments, the one on the French female prisoners of war at Ravensbrück, and the one on Auschwitz.

I seem to remember that my mother had bought the volumes from a door-to-door salesman who sold collections of books around the countryside where we lived; we'd also gotten from him a complete and rather unsophisticated leather-bound collection of Zola, whose volumes were so heavy they made my wrists buckle.

They left me with aches that never faded.

THE LEMON YOGURTS

In the family-sized variety packs of flavored yogurts always came four containers of lemon; it must have been a relic of some old French culinary tradition, perpetuated, I believe, by the sadism of industrial statistics.

We freely ate all of the other flavors, but unfortunately, when only lemon-flavored yogurts remained, my father still felt that we had yogurt.

And when the lemon yogurts stayed in the fridge for too long, he'd systematically hand them out at the end of the meal as if they were dessert.

I ate everything from cauliflower, salsify, broccoli, and chard, to brains, liver, cod liver oil, and cod liver oil, but I could *not* eat those lemon yogurts.

My brothers consumed them as one consumes a vegetable recommended for good health.

I, on another hand, experienced an immediate and total paralysis.

(37)

But my brothers had pity. So they reflected quite a bit on a solution to save me (though, I will note that they preferred to take ridiculous risks, rather than simply eating my serving of lemon yogurt).

My father never ate dessert and often left the room.

During some dull sojourn at the lunch table one day, my brother reached his hands behind the tablecloth that hung down, then up under the big table, and felt a drawer under the tray.

And it was there that he quickly emptied my lemon yogurt. The three of us, him included, shot incredulous glances around the room and held our breaths. Nothing happened.

On later occasions, we would add a few little pieces of chewy meat and ham fat here and there.

A quiet routine was established until, one day, the tension surrounding mealtimes reappeared in a completely bewildering way when our stepmother said:

"What is that smell?"

She sniffed her way closer to the table.

She called my father. They began circling the table.

THE SWITCHBOARD

Now about "La Chauffe," well, it was always one of the Residents who gave us a ride. And the Bar too was tended by a Resident. And it was also a Resident who managed the switchboard.

"Hello, La Borde, I'm listening. Please stay on the line—" *beep-beep beep-beep beep-beep beep-beep*

"Yes, with whom would you like to speak?"

"Nicole Perdreau. She's in the Medical Coordinator's Office."

"Who's on the line?"

"Her daughter."

"Please stay on the line—" *beep-beep beep-beep beep-beep*

"She's not at the MCO right now. Shall I try the Castle's Infirmary?"

"No, she's probably on the ground floor—" *beep-beep beep-beep beep-beep*

"No one's answering. I'll try the Park—" *beep-beep beep-beep*

"I'm told she just left for the Extension. I'll try her there, please stay on the line—" *beep-beep beep-beep beep-beep*

"She's not at the Extension's Infirmary either, please stay on the line—" *beep-beep beep-beep*

"…"

We squirmed hysterically by the phone booth that ate our coins.

RÉGILAIT MILK

My father never bought fresh milk. Instead, he stocked it, always keeping a huge tin of Régilait powdered milk (an odd habit he'd kept from the war and from his grandparents' family business).

It reigned in the pantry like some menacing totem with loud colors. Monday mornings, he prepared our hot chocolates in a pan with that pragmatic milk choice. We watched the whole process from our position, piled on the bench.

The little clink of the bowl being laid on the table in front of me sucked the air out of the room. And then my father would step out again to fetch his satchel from his office.

We counted his steps. As soon as we heard him rummaging about his papers, one of my brothers would grab my bowl, hand it to my other brother, who, having gotten up, would step over the bench, rush to the front door, and toss the chocolate out in the flower beds, then return and seat himself the second my father reappeared. The rose bush eventually collapsed and died from the poor quality of the Sologne soil—according to my stepmother's conjectures.

PARIS–VIERZON

A cold heavy rain pours out of the dark grey sky. I'm running along, half drowning under these enormous bulky drops; I'm running along the tall hedge and its low horizon, along the little footpath that borders the lawn; I tuck in my head to protect my face; you can't see a thing anyway. I can only barely make out the white clot that is the Castle.

I steer myself toward the entrance to the Kitchen.

I have almost reached the end of the alleyway when I sense a presence to my right.

There's someone here.

It's impossible, it's raining so hard. It would be insane to stand here, but then again, it might be a Madman. Who knows.

Oh well, I've got no choice but to run past him.

I'd rather not get hit. Oh well. I can't go into the grass with my pretty little shoes.

It's a man in a beige raincoat with a hat on.

He is holding his collar, propped up on both sides, over his chin. I cannot distinguish his face.

But he must be out of his mind, just standing there like that! We're the only two still outside.

As I draw close, he suddenly untucks his head and calls to me in a whisper:

"Manou!"

Paralysis. It's my father!

He catches me by the arm and pulls me over to the side.

Out of instinct, I peer once more toward the stoop of the Castle a few meters beyond the pretty white gravel.

We are trapped inside the small cage of the rain.

I can't think of anything to say to him other than:

"But Daddy, what are you doing here?"

He pulls his collar up higher and, looking around conspicuously, says in an impatient whisper:

"Shush, not so loud. I came here *incognito*."

"But, Daddy, you're dead!"

He breaks into laughter and then makes a little scornful sound:

"Pff!"

"But Daddy, what are we going to do? We sold your apartment, we don't have your things anymore, you have no more money! What are you going to do?"

He looks around again and says:
"I'm going to rebuild my life in Vierzon."

Then, another *pff!*, and he marches off into an opaque curtain of rain; I see a section of his back drawing away.

I run toward the Castle.

II

THE THREE ROLLOVERS

The car rolled over three times. My mother was holding me in her arms and curled up like a hedgehog.

We had no seatbelts; they didn't exist back then.

Eventually, all of us got out through different windows. We were in a muddy field. After all the commotion, the car stayed on its roof.

One, two, three, four, my father screams:

"James!"

He hears cries and rushes forward. My brother tugs on the little vest of his cowboy outfit, which is smoking, caught underneath the burning hot motor.

"We'll buy you a new one."

The farmers working the field appear. She is wearing a floral print blouse against her naked legs. Children have come too.

No one's hurt. The car is a sorry sight.

"Come in and use the phone," the lady says.

We're in this farmhouse kitchen. There is a table with four chairs, a formica dresser, and tiles on the floor.

Dumb city-slickers.

Don't know a thing.

The woman pours us each a glass of milk.

My brother refuses to drink it, and snorts, headstrong.

When it's time to leave, the fat fly drowned inside his glass has risen to the surface.

THE ALGERIAN WAR

My mother has just given birth. The Algerian War is raging. Those were the times of the 'suitcase carriers.'

Someone arrives out of breath to warn my father: the police are on their way.

There's some commotion in the house. My father shoves some documents into my mother's hands—*Hide this!*—and rushes out onto the stoop.

My mother grabs my baby brother. She rushes into the bedroom and locks herself in. A policeman knocks on the door. Then enters. My brother is crimson: he hollers in anger. My mother bounces him on her shoulder, walking in circles around the room. He is uttering furious high-pitched screams. She is in a floral bathrobe, yellow and spongy like a woman in labor.

My father is pale as a sheet; he gawks at my mother.

They search everywhere, in the cupboards, in the drawers, to the soundtrack of the baby's screams. Everyone's nervous.

The policemen leave.

My father is baffled.

"I lined James's diapers with the lists," my mother explains, opening my brother's diaper.

THE LOIR

We are drifting along in a small bark on the deliciously fresh Loir. The foliage weaves like a trellis above our heads and the trunks offer us their cooling shade.

Our parents are rowing at a hearteningly synchronized pace. We let our hands drag in the water. There is a slight smell of sludge and of green water.

We are in the world of the river; it's a point of view on things, we exist differently here, carried along by the current, and with it, drawing a thin slit into the thick body of reality.

A deep sense of wellbeing comes over us. Far off, behind the curve, the sublime ruins of the Lavardin donjon appears. Suddenly, my mother cries out, panicked:

"I forgot to turn off the stove under the pot of water!"

Dismay.

She whimpers.

"The house is surely on fire!"

In the middle of the river, we are all now in the heart of the fire.

My father, energetically spinning us around with a paddle, says:

"Back to the car."

She answers:

"But it will be too late!"

We're overcome with a sense of urgency. We row nervously. We move toward the shore. The entangled branches and fat roots on the bank are now our enemy, blocking our access to the edge. My mother clings to a branch. The bark sways. We are all afraid. My mother writhes; she's on the embankment, then starts running through the fields.

THE RAT

We are piled in a corner of the big room, grouped around the television's black and white screen.

The heating is powerless. The room is enormous.

A small distance from me, a rat crosses the wood floor.

"Oh, a rat," I utter thoughtlessly.

My father leaps to a prodigious height (despite his lack of athleticism).

"Where?" he roars.

"Over there! It's under the radiator!"

My father runs into the kitchen to seize the broom and, in a flash, his sword is clashing against the cast-iron.

We stand around him; we can see the back of the abused creature bucking with all its might. And suddenly, we see its little nose and gleaming eyes.

In four little leaps, the rat has climbed up the broomstick and hurled itself at my father's eyes.

My father drops everything.

I cannot remember how we ended up breaking the rat's back, or if we threw it outside, or both.

"It's my glasses that saved me," my father declares.

MONSIEUR BELIN

Monsieur Belin would take me with him to pick asparagus.

First, seated at the table in the lingering night, he'd have bread and salami, coffee, and a glass of wine.

As soon as the sun was up, I'd be waiting seated in a chair, ready to go.

In the Belin household, you had to brush your teeth before breakfast.

He'd go outside and come back in with a big wicker basket. Standing on the stoop with his muddy boots, he'd grab me and place me in the basket.

I held on for a bit with my hands, watching the outline of Madame Belin behind us in a square of light, like the image of some saint. Monsieur Belin owned a field near his house, just across the road. That's where he grew asparagus.

The field was perfectly brown (and dusty in summer). Little lumps covered its expanse.

Like the even undulations of a very organized sea. Monsieur Belin called them 'the rows.'

He'd tell me in his nasal voice:

"I'll set you here so you can see me."

Bent like a hairpin, he'd harrow each bulge of earth and move farther and farther away after arranging each one.

I stayed in the basket, all wrapped up, my gaze set on Monsieur Belin's extraordinarily shrinking silhouette.

When he grew too small, I'd utter a brief cry:

"Eeeeeeeee!"

He'd toss some words at me in the misty grey:

"I'm coming."

He'd come back with his bowed-legged stride, weighed down by the mud.

And would place himself at the start of a new row.

THE FROZEN TILES

After the cradle and the bassinet, they moved me into the big bed.

The furniture belonged to Belin's parents. It was a bedroom set fit for a farmhouse, chosen to last a lifetime of honor and virtue. Something dignified. The linens were always immaculate, perfectly seemly. A dark green and padded sateen bed cover, pulled taught, tied the whole look together. It smelled a little like naphthalene, which, in that frigid room, endowed the bed with yet more solemnity (and even, as I noticed some years later, with a look of cadaveric stiffness, or called to mind the custom mausoleums presented in funeral homes).

At my age though, it had been of no importance. Instead, what shaped my perception of the place were the violent tremors that surged through me with each step I took along the cold maroon tiles, which Monsieur Belin had used to cover the floor. Belin had added a hallway, made mysterious by its length, with the very same tiles, to connect this extension back to the main house. Mornings and evenings, crossing it proved a stupefying physiological experiment for my tiny feet.

Back then, well, at least at the beginning, they left me a little chamber pot by the bed for the night. The cabin—the privy—was at somewhat of a distance in the garden, so we only went there during the day.

Later, Belin converted the pigsty into a bathroom, connecting us to modern comforts in a flash. He tiled it with the same tiles, a visual prompt that evoked the promised sensation each step would bring. I still remember the paralyzing icy burn that crept up my spine in small shockwaves until it reached my head.

I left the Belin household before they had installed a heater.

The wood stove, with its three little metallic doors, provided much of the entertainment. The little furnace of the boiler, cracked open next to me with a thousand precautions, was like a carpet of incandescent rubies. I stood by it surrounded by words of warning.

We ate soup. Well, the Belins ate, and I spoke incessantly:

"The teacher said…" "The teacher did…"

Madame Belin withered away behind her patient exterior.

"Eat now, Manou."

Kind as she was, she never forced me to finish.

She had a set of decorated dishes: vegetables would float along the edges of one plate, a still life of vegetables would lie in the center of another. I preferred some designs to others.

Belin would bring me a plate that was full to the brim, and the only way for me to discover the design of the day was to eat everything. That lasted a while, the time it took for me to learn all of the different combinations: a radish on the top left and a carrot on the right meant it was the plate with the cabbage, tomato, and turnip bouquet.

At La Borde, there were no such things. We ate out of Pyrex plates—sometimes they were maroon, sometimes transparent.

Belin also bought me alphabet pasta, to cheer me up, and get me to reach the bottom of the soup (once immersed in the hot liquid, the pasta became heavy and rebelled against my spoon). It was good, but to eat the letters I first had to sip down all of the soup, lips pinched. I gathered up the letters on the side of the plate. Once I was finally able to spell something, the broth was cold, I was no longer hungry, and we'd all give up.

We'd go to bed early because Monsieur Belin would pick asparagus in the mornings before going off to work at the Clinic.

At La Borde, there were Madmen whom we called 'Residents.' I have always found that word elegant. It's a long word. And how mysterious, that Daudet's Monsieur Seguin had a 'resident' in his backyard as well.

I also liked the word Permanence (the office responsible for "La Chauffe," which provided our daily ride). I liked to say, "He is at the *Permanence.*" When someone was *de permanence*, they were on call or on duty. We'd ask, "Who is manning the *Permanence* today?" And sometimes, ironically, the *Permanence* was closed.

The Madmen of La Borde too seemed eternal. Certain even kept a smooth face; my father used to say: great madness keeps you young.

Did the Madmen scare us? Not all of them, at least not more than regular people. With some of them, however, it would have been extremely reckless not to be careful. Were we ashamed of them? I discovered Opera while making my way down the staircase of the Clinic one day, where I could hear an air that was being sung in the Grand Salon: *Softly awakes my heart, as the flowers awaken.*

Did we consider it strange for there to be so many Madmen per square foot, in our vicinity? At La Borde, they only took care of grown Madmen; there were no mad children. Did that mean we thought we'd end up sounding like Madmen when we grew up?

My mother was born in '37. In 1945, she'd still never eaten cake. Until the end of the war, there'd always been something missing: eggs, sugar, or cream.

When rationing ended in 1947, she finally ate one. "I don't like cake," she'd said.

She tells us the acorn story. How they'd ran out of coffee. Then how the girls had braved the winter in the woods, in the snow with their clogs on, to find acorns (like some little rodents). Petrified, how they'd picked the acorns. How it was forbidden, a bit like in the Middle Ages. How they'd filled the basket anyway. How it'd been an amazing harvest. How they were proud like children. And then the story takes the turn of dark fable. A tall German man appears, like the wolf. He asks the girls:

"What are you doing?"

They tell him.

He takes the basket, and dumps their reaping lickety-split.

He returns the basket to the children, and chases them away.

THE MEAT

For some minutes now, we have been peering, stunned, and reluctant, at the pieces of meat set on our plates.

Our stepmother detects our heretic behavior during one of her trips back into the kitchen.

She draws closer, slim in her miniskirt, with her wooden spatula still in her hand, and finally says:

"Come on! Eat!"

Sighs.

"You're really starting to be a nuisance," she yelps.

"Your meat smells like shit," my brother suddenly intones like some baritone.

Our stepmother's jaw drops open and our father's name slips out.

My brother leaves the table lifted up by his collar.

No investigation. But in the upheaval, no one remembers to make us eat the meat.

THE BELL

We've just settled in Vaugoin. On a few dozen hectares with a castle, which is on the far side of the property, and of which we occupy one wing.

My father has gone to work at La Borde. We are spending the afternoon with my stepmother.

We disappear to play in the forest.

Evening comes. My father makes his way back slowly: two yellow circles of light oscillating along the long drive full of potholes.

There is a bell on the wall near the door of the castle, with a chain somewhat concealed by the Virginia creeper. Just as we are accustomed to at La Borde, where the bell is rung to call the residents in for dinner, my stepmother pulls the chain three times and returns inside the house.

We run back; we sit down to eat.

Suddenly, a knock on the door.

We answer. It's the owner.

Behind him, half of the townspeople, who have come carrying buckets, and tubs, to put out the fire.

We had accidentally rung the old fire bell.

THE APPOINTMENT WITH LACAN

It's summer in Paris. My stepmother has an appointment. She parks her car along the Quai Malaquais.

She tells me: "I'll be back."

I see her walking away through the rear window of her Mini.

Now she's talking to Lacan:

"Bla, bla, bla... the children, yes, there are three of them, they make things a bit rough for me, they come over every weekend, and for half the holidays; as a matter of fact, I can't stay long, the little one's waiting."

"Pardon?"

"She's waiting for me in the car."

"..."

"She's not alone. The dog's with her."

"..."

"I locked the door."

A moment later, Lacan is chattering with me, and giving me some crayons to draw with.

Whenever we went up to Paris, my brother would have prepared an entire schedule ahead of time. He'd set his shoes on his bed. The night before the trip, he'd keep me awake by hurling them at me, so he could finish presenting all of his great ideas. Of course, it only worked twice.

At the time, our age difference bore a certain consequence. I remember the superhuman effort I'd have to make to stay awake, and answer him with little sounds, and dying onomatopoeias, until silence finally betrayed me, and the shoe thrust me back at once into my role of listener.

One exceptionally sun-bleached afternoon, we are driving toward Thoiry. My father has explained to us that it is a park where African animals roam freely.

We drive slowly through an opening in the woods. It's very flat. We stop. There are lions. It's very hot, which completes the picture well. The lions circum-navigate the car, which they sniff. They walk off. It's very hot.

Farther off, on great slow legs, a group of giraffes walks by at eye level. The stark contrasts of their coats is very elegant. They seem to like us; they draw nearer. They circle the car, one of them spreads its front paws in an odd fashion, and brings its face closer to the opening of the window. My brothers and I, as though a single being, fall upon each other like a small accordion in the back-bench. The giraffe comes closer and closer still. My stepmother screams; my father cries out:

"Roll up the window!"

Her gigantic head is now in the car; she performs an agile twist and seizes the straw hat sitting on the back deck, chews it up, and retires.

My father is waiting for dinner to end. He removes his glasses and, rumpling his eyes with his fingers, says:

"Aren't you going to eat your chicken bones?"

One time, a friend we'd had over for dinner had taken him so seriously that he had started chomping on his banana peel.

OUTSPAN ORANGES

Our childhood wore itself out among the grown-ups. We didn't understand much of anything. Like sleepwalkers, through all of the chatter and the thick layers of cigarette smoke.

We weren't the focus; but we'd been quite used to that at La Borde.

Various political messages intoned by posters or magazine covers in Vaugoin would grip my imagination (especially since they were never taken down, and were featured in places where we often went, even several times a day).

I'd contemplate them for hours in private.

There was the issue of *Hara Kiri* that read, *What are kids dreaming about today? To chow down on adults.*[1]

There was the poster denouncing Outspan, henchman, arm of the apartheid, and which featured a little

---

1. Que veulent les jeunes? Bouffer les vieux.

black boy whose head was being squeezed into an orange-press by a giant white hand (and which forever soured the taste of orange juice for me; not to mention the doubts that blood oranges elicited in me after that). And then there was the MLF poster, which, in brief, assured the world that if contraception and abortion weren't made legal, well, women would keep having children until they started having monsters.

Our kitchen turned red. I liked it; it brought a certain carmine peace, but I understood how it was, well, somewhat innovative.

The life of others seemed rather quiet to me. In their white kitchens.

We were living a sweeping transformation, a dynamic new modern age.

However, a cunning or perhaps pathetic presence remained—the insistent refrain of our grandparents' values, left stranded in our present by some past esthetic—and took the shape of the paintings, beds, and ancient armoires which roamed about our lives. The past was peppered inside the décor in small touches, wedged between modern items of furniture like holograms from a different world.

That furniture, and those objects, left me with the same malaise I felt from old photographs where the pictured individual's outdated costume weakens the empathy in the viewer's gaze, loosens the ties of our humanity, and prevents us from acknowledging the slow fading that awaits us all.

And the war, like the wallpaper, was an eternal backdrop to the family stories told by grandparents, uncles, and aunts.

It seemed that one of the wars crushed the other; the Second World War erased the Great War. Of the two narratives, one of them faded like the voice of seniors. After our grandfather's death, there was nothing left of 1914 but his infamous handkerchiefs and their memories of mustard gas. We'd speak of it at dinnertime. We'd say:

"He was gassed, first, with mustard gas. And then he was trepanned. Could you pass me the dish, please?"

Over time, the mere mention of "grandfather's handkerchiefs," was enough for everyone to get the idea.

1940 took on a greater significance (even though we hadn't fought in it).

My aunt Jeannine would tell this story:

"One day, at the mill, we were fired at by an airplane; Pop made us run around the trees."

"Pop ran guns. In a crate on the back of his bicycle, under the potatoes. One day, the Germans stopped us along the road. I threw my bike on the floor and ran toward pop's legs. The sulfate sprayer lay on top of the potatoes, which were above the disassembled rifles. They asked him what it was, and Pop said: "A doryphore sprayer." They rung up their captain. I thought they were going to shoot us on the spot; but they only yelled because we'd said "doryphores."[2]

"Everyone at home cried when the war was declared."

2. *Doryphores*, potato bugs, was a slang word for Germans during the war.

She'd also tell us:

"Spaniards slept in our house, under the table. In the Chambord Forest, there were many Spaniards."

"At the Moulin de Clénord, an old German man brought us chocolate."

"Jandeau denounced a neighbor to the Blois Gestapo."

"On D-Day, the French Forces of the Interior went to pick him up. My uncle says they ran him into the Russy Forest, and that he fled through the vines, like a rabbit. They tracked him like an animal. They killed him there in the vines."

THE NOUVELLES GALERIES

One Monday, Fazia and I are moseying around the big department store in the center of town. I swipe something. We are leaving when suddenly somebody grips my braids and pulls hard.

Fazia runs off.

"Open your hand," a woman orders me.

"What an ill-mannered customer," she mumbles over and over, to her left, to her right, while nodding her head, and pushing me along toward the back of the store.

She holds onto my wrist very firmly.

I'm sitting in the administrative offices. I'm waiting to see a manager.

The manager ends up calling my parents. He hands me my father.

"I'm coming," is all he says, but without anger.

I wait for a while.

He arrives. He says:

"How much do I owe you?"
We leave.
We're in the car. He tells me:
"Here's that little pendant, take it."
And adds:
"You're not going to hang yourself, are you?"

THE ENGUERRAND BROTHERS

A mysterious triptych of a single mind, the Enguerrand brothers walked along with their hands in their pockets.

Like the hieratic altarpiece of the same figure, the eldest had a beard, the middle one some fancy lace in place of syntax, carried by a little falsetto voice, and the youngest bit the corner of his closed lips while listening silently.

I learned to eat soup just before dining at their house. Their grandmother always came over for lunch. Simon whispered to me:

"Let me show you: fill your spoon, sip only half of it, and most importantly, make sure you never bang the spoon against the bottom of the plate." (He'd kick me in the shin when I made a mistake.)

The Enguerrand brothers were a gang unto themselves, they were like the opening scene of a Western, like the Dalton brothers, but way better.

The middle one was the prettiest. Gabriel was the mascot of the Blois girls. He was delicate and graceful, and the way he presented himself as a boy was quiet and introverted. He had a delicious dimple that made Isabelle go crazy.

Yet, the one I liked the most was the youngest one. He was my age, though that wasn't why I liked him.

He said 'chat' instead of 'talk'; we 'chatted' a lot together.

We had things in common.

I learned that beyond the big forest, there was a castle with Madmen and that some children lived there too.

At first, he'd come over for no reason, after school, taking the shortcut through the woods on his bicycle to get to my house; he'd be terribly red when he arrived. He'd stand in front of the white fence, unsaddled, hip tipped off his bike. I'd come out with a glass of water. We were incapable of exchanging a single word. He would drink, and leave.

One day, my mother got angry:

"At your age, love doesn't exist!"

We'd known La Borde's car cemetery.

The Enguerrand Brothers had their father's vast car collection. They drove around like princes in those old automobiles.

Once his legs had gotten long enough, around nine years old, Simon started to learn how to drive. I did too. But I was still too short and writhed about like some gimp on those pedals with the dashboard at the level of my eyes.

(86)

THE YOUNG STAG

We're off to catch the bus to high school. I'm walking behind Anne. She's sulking; it's too early for her to be in a good mood, and the hot water had run out in the shower. When we reach the right spot on the lawn, in front of the Chambord Castle, we enter into a thick swath of mist hanging off the ground; I see only the wet and rumpled grass ahead of my feet, spread unevenly about the cold earth. Anne's ankles, a few meters ahead of me, flutter slightly. She is bodiless and headless. She has disappeared, completely engulfed by the humid cloud. I call her. I hear a warm breath, very close, off to my left:

Rawwwwwwwwr

"Get down!" Anne yelps.

I fall to the ground like a heavy sack.

Rawwwwwwwwr

I see two delicate, slender paws, then four, and then little black split hooves. The young stag pauses, then resumes his journey, navigating through the mist.

ABOUT THE AUTHOR

Emmanuelle Guattari was born in 1964. She grew up at the La Borde psychiatric clinic (at Cour-Cheverny, in the Loir-et-Cher, France) where her parents worked for their entire lives. She has taught French and English in the United States and in France. She now devotes herself to writing. She has three children and lives in Paris. *I, Little Asylum* is her first novel.